# In the Cab

By Debbie Croft

Cam is in the cab.

Cam has a hat.

The hat fits Cam.

hat

cab

Cam sits in the cab.

The cab has a map.

Cam can see the map.

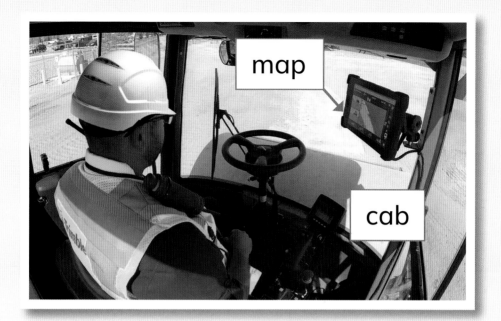

Cam rips at the pit.

He sits in the cab and rips.

cab

*Rip, rip, rip!*

Cam sits in the cab.

He can tip.

Cam tips at the pit.

# CHECKING FOR MEANING

1. Where does Cam sit? *(Literal)*

2. What does Cam do at the pit? *(Literal)*

3. Why do you think there is a map in the cab? *(Inferential)*

# EXTENDING VOCABULARY

| | |
|---|---|
| **cab** | What does the word *cab* mean? Explain that sometimes *cab* is used as a short form of the word *cabin*. |
| **hat** | What other words rhyme with *hat*? Use one in a sentence to show what the word means. |
| **map** | Look at the word *map* in the text. What does a *map* help us do? |

# MOVING BEYOND THE TEXT

1. What big machine is Cam sitting in?

2. What other machines or vehicles have a cab?

3. Why is Cam tipping dirt into a truck?

4. Do you think Cam enjoys his work? How do you know?

## SPEED SOUNDS

| Cc | Bb | Rr | Ee | Ff | Hh | Nn |
|----|----|----|----|----|----|----|
| Mm | Ss | Aa | Pp | Ii | Tt | |

# PRACTICE WORDS

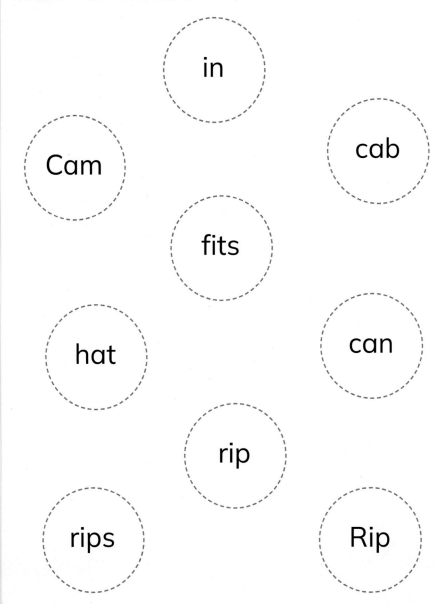

in

Cam

cab

fits

hat

can

rip

rips

Rip